Picasso in Mougins, 1970

Picasso's work between the wars was marked by inexhaustible and innovative stylistic alternations: adopting a Cubist style on one painting using ever purer geometrical abstraction, then the swelling forms of the voluminous neoclassicist style, or again, dramatic and expressive deformations

Unerschöpflicher innovativer Wechsel kennzeichnet die Zwischenkriegszeit: Hier ein Kubismus der immer reineren geometrischen Abstraktion, dort die schwellenden Formen eines voluminösen Neoklassizismus, da dramatisch-ausdrucksstarke Deformationen in Nähe zum Surrealismus.

18 detachable postcards
18 Postkarten zum Heraustrennen

approaching Surrealism. The year 1937, in which Picasso painted *Guernica*, depicting the horrific vision of Franco's despotism, was also the year in which he produced his most enchanting portraits of women. And the late work unleashes a veritable flood of merry, elegiac, tender, bucolic, resplendently erotic scenes. In the second half of his life, alongside his paintings and drawings, the incomparable artist created no less rich and virtuoso sculptures, ceramics, and prints.

Biographical data

Born on October 25, 1881, in Málaga (Andalusia), 1895–97 studies art in Barcelona and Madrid. Visits Paris for the first time in 1901; moves there in 1904. From 1923 also lives in Antibes, from 1949 in Vallauris, from 1958 in the château at Vauvenargues. Joins the Communist Party in 1944. Several marriages and relationships, four children. The Picasso Museum in Barcelona opens in 1963. Dies on April 8, 1973, in Mougins. Buried in Vauvenargues.

1937, das Jahr des Schrekkensbildes der Franco-Willkür, ›Guernica‹, ist zugleich ein Jahr der zauberhaftesten mehransichtigen Frauenporträts. Und das Spätwerk entfesselt einen wahren Strom heiterer, elegischer, zärtlicher, bukolischer, prangend erotischer Paar-Szenerien. In der zweiten Hälfte seines Lebens schuf der große Bildermacher parallel zur Malerei und Zeichnung nicht minder reiche und virtuose Werkgruppen an Bildhauerei, Keramik und Druckgraphik.

Lebensdaten

Geboren am 25. Oktober 1881 in Malaga (Andalusien). 1895–97 Kunststudium in Barcelona und Madrid. Ab 1901 zeitweise, ab 1904 ständig in Paris. Daneben Ateliers im Süden, seit 1923 in Antibes, ab 1949 in Vallauris, von 1958 an auf Schloß Vauvenargues. 1944 Eintritt in die KP. Mehrere Ehen und Partnerschaften, vier Kinder. 1963 Picasso-Museum in Barcelona eröffnet. Gestorben am 8. April 1973 in Mougins. Grab in Vauvenargues.

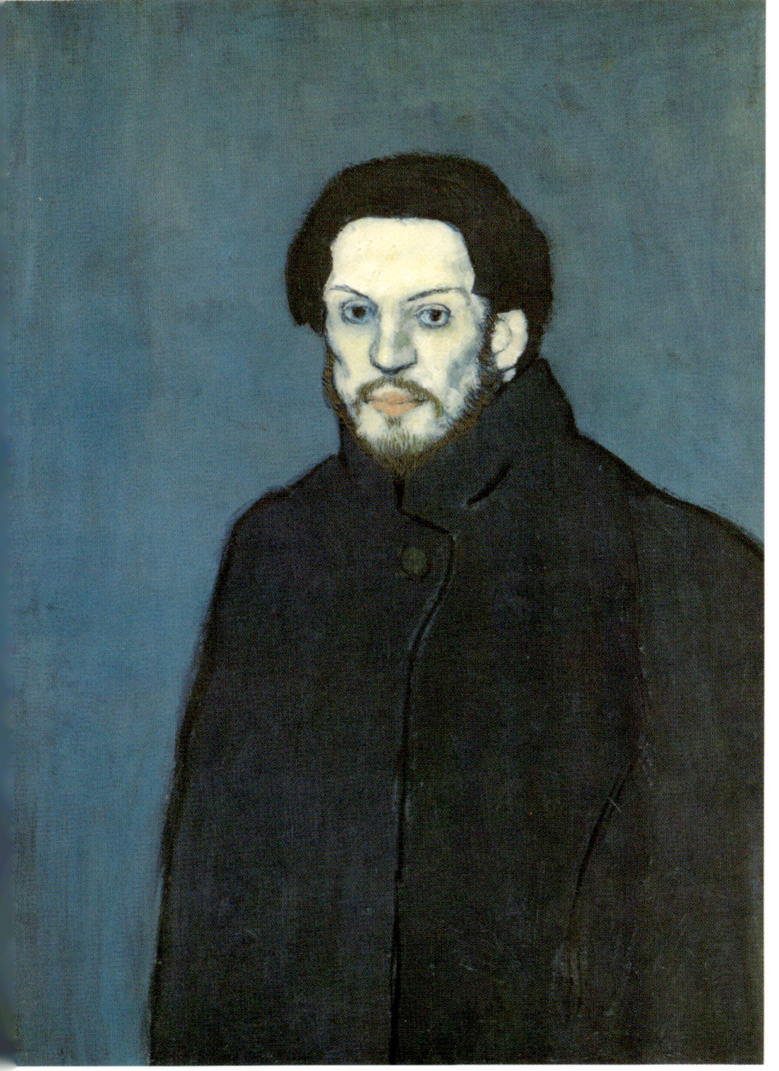

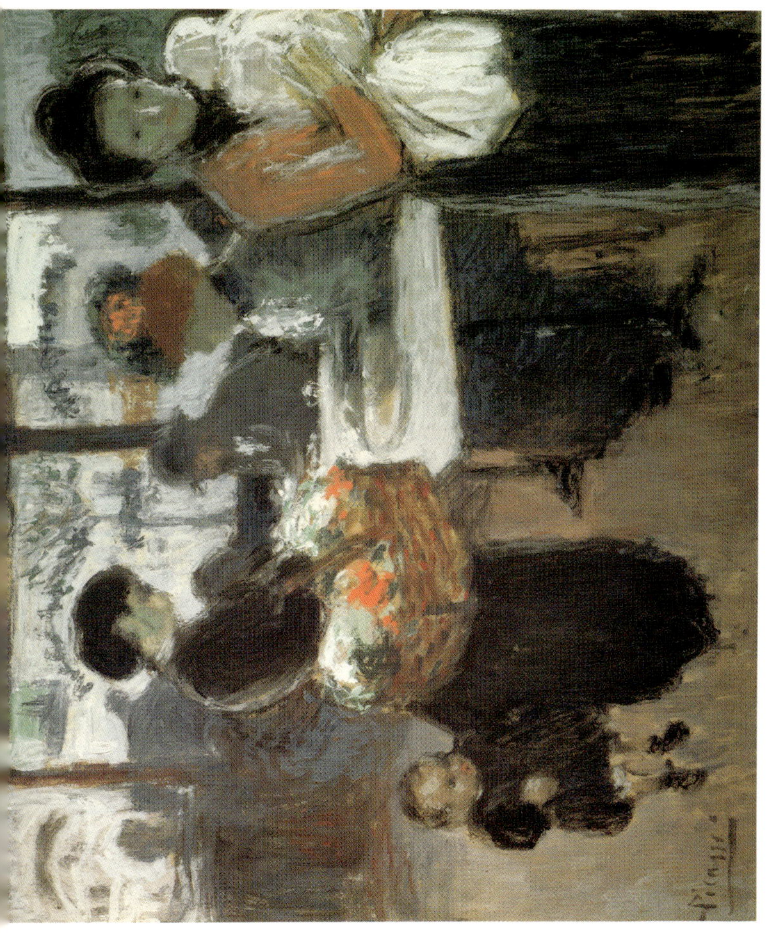

Pablo Picasso
Café in Montmartre/Café am Montmartre, 1901
© Succession Picasso/VG Bild-Kunst, Bonn, 1993. Museum Ludwig, Cologne

From the Prestel book/Aus dem Prestel-Buch:
Picasso, The Ludwig Collection/Die Sammlung Ludwig
(English and German editions) Prestel, Munich · New York

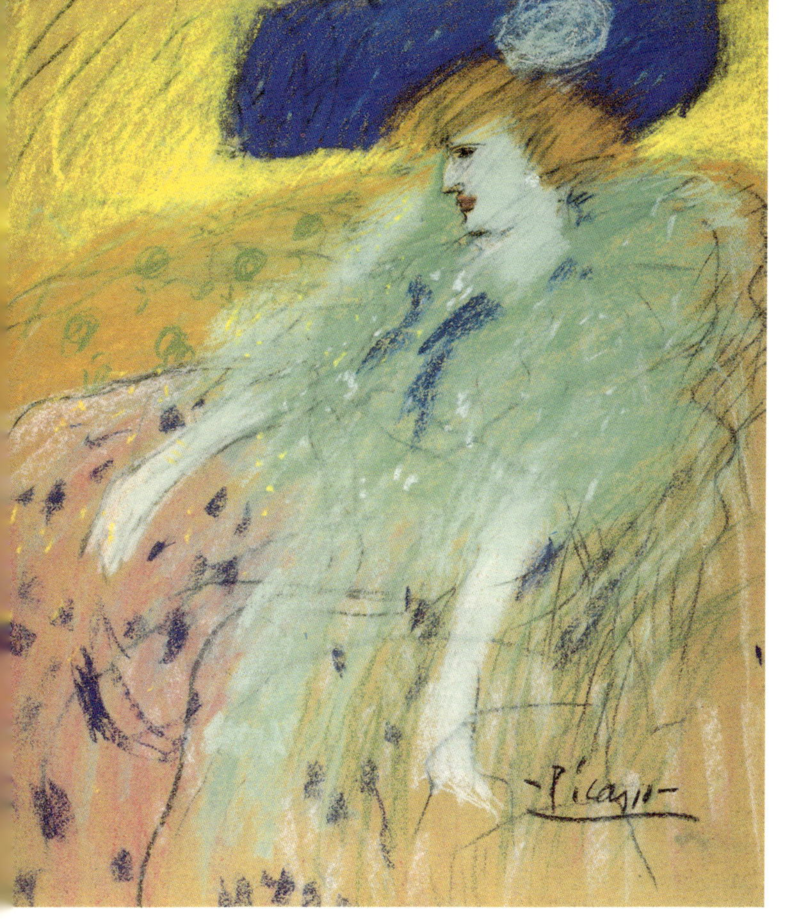
-Picasso-

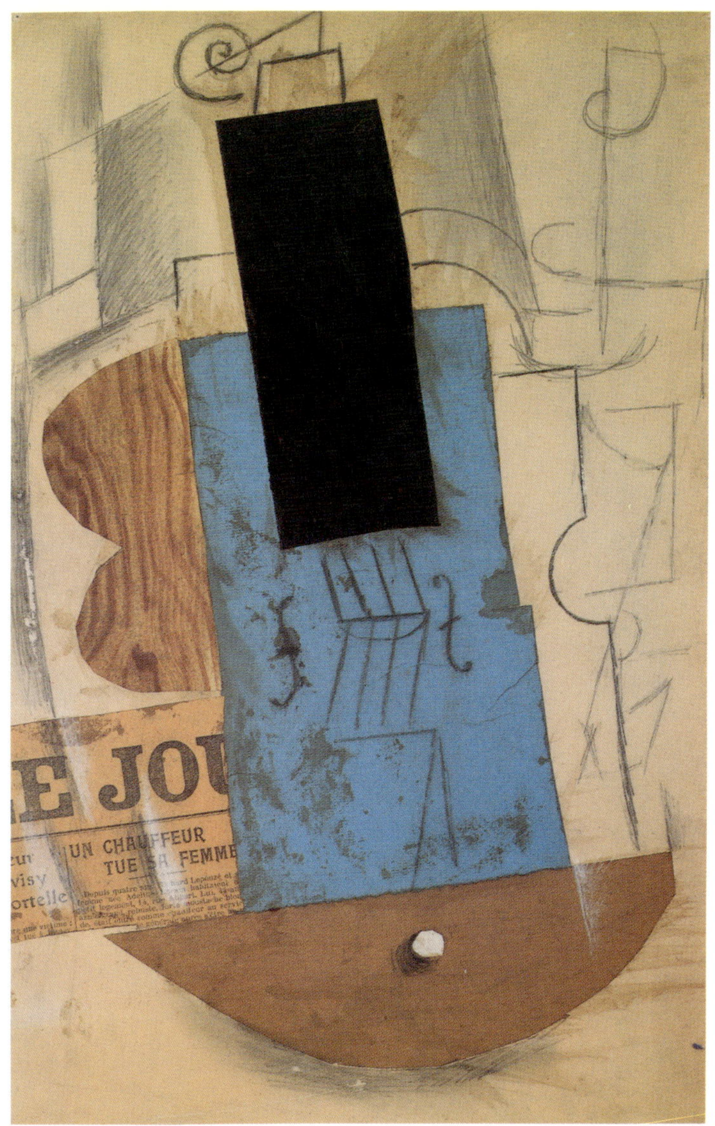
E JOU
UN CHAUFFEUR
TUE SA FEMME
visy
ortelle

Pablo Picasso
Still Life with Newspaper and Violin/Stilleben mit Zeitung und Violine, 1912
© Succession Picasso/VG Bild-Kunst, Bonn, 1993. Museum Ludwig, Cologne

From the Prestel book/Aus dem Prestel-Buch:
Picasso, The Ludwig Collection/Die Sammlung Ludwig
(English and German editions) Prestel, Munich · New York

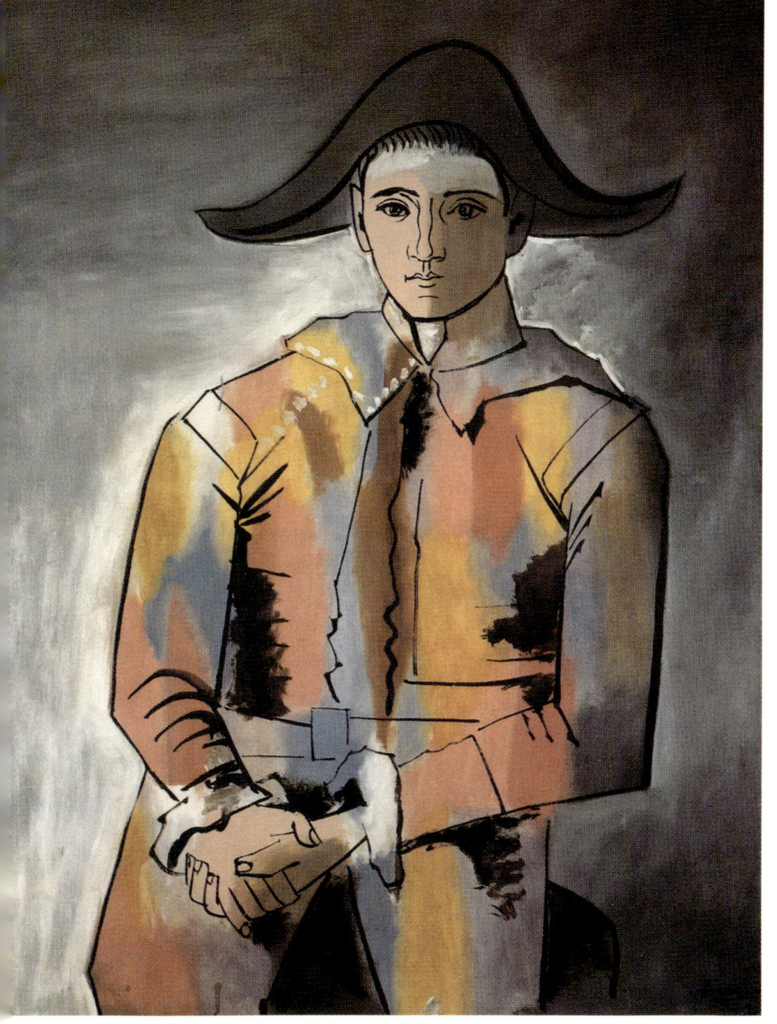

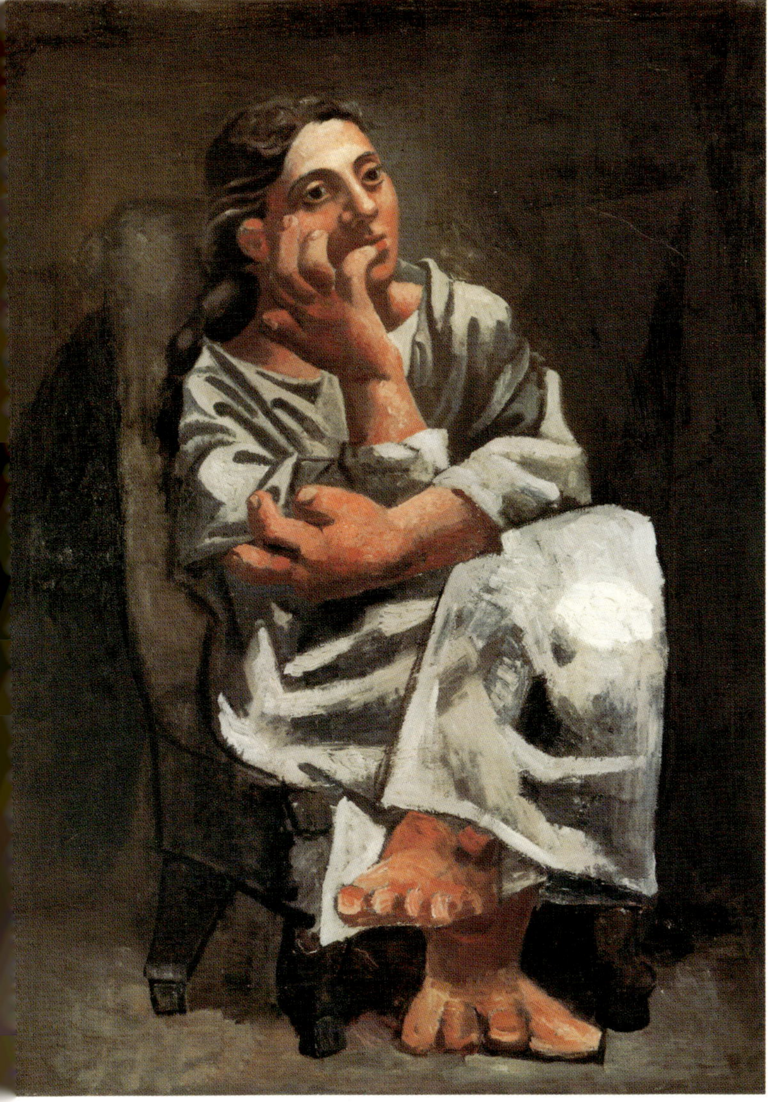

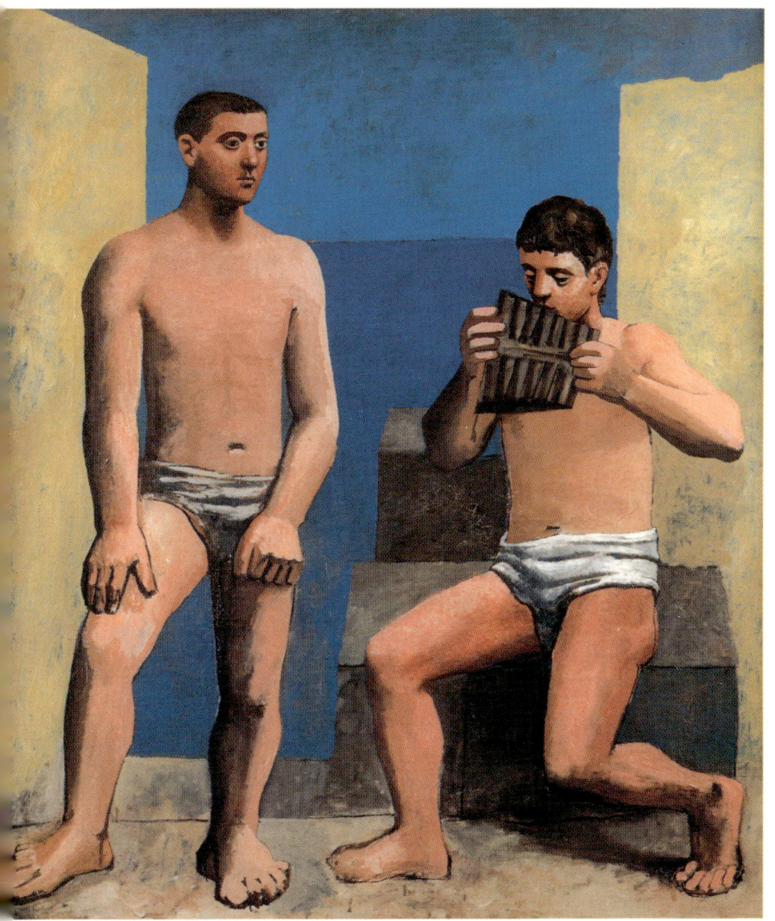

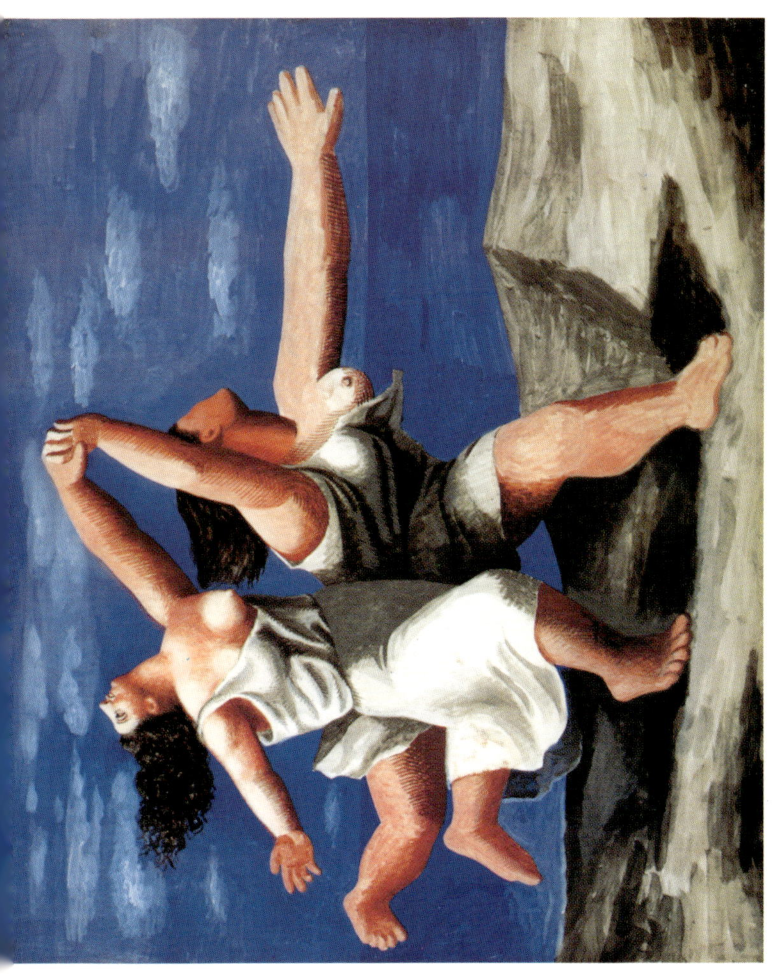

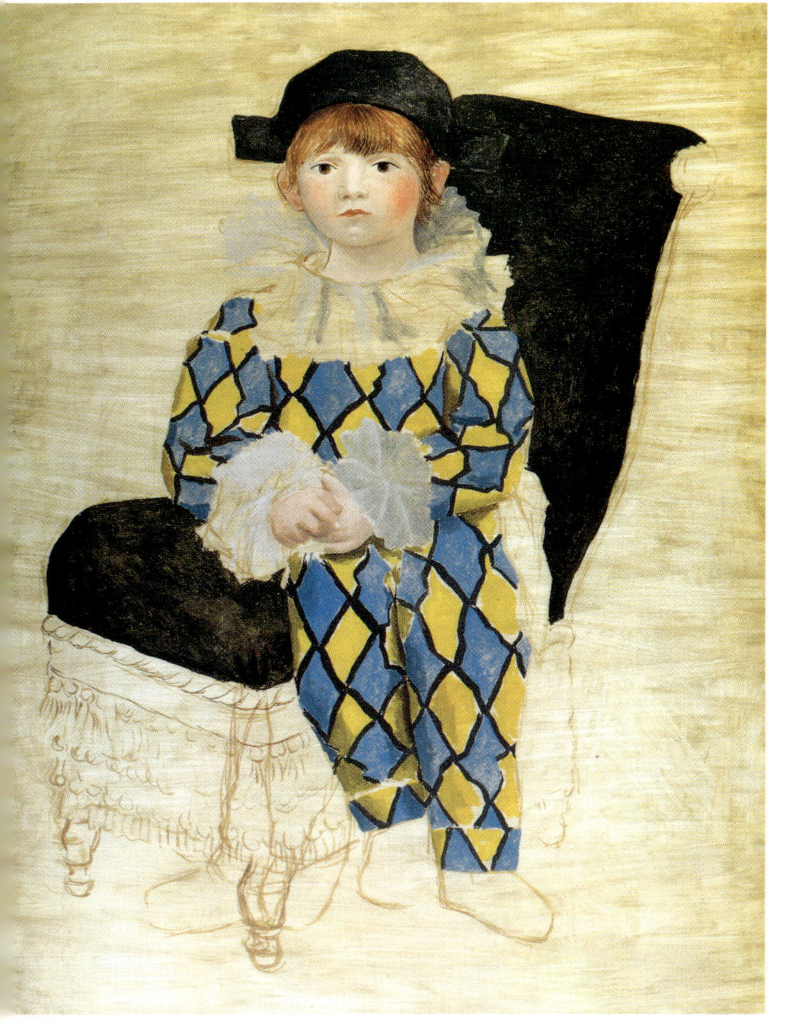

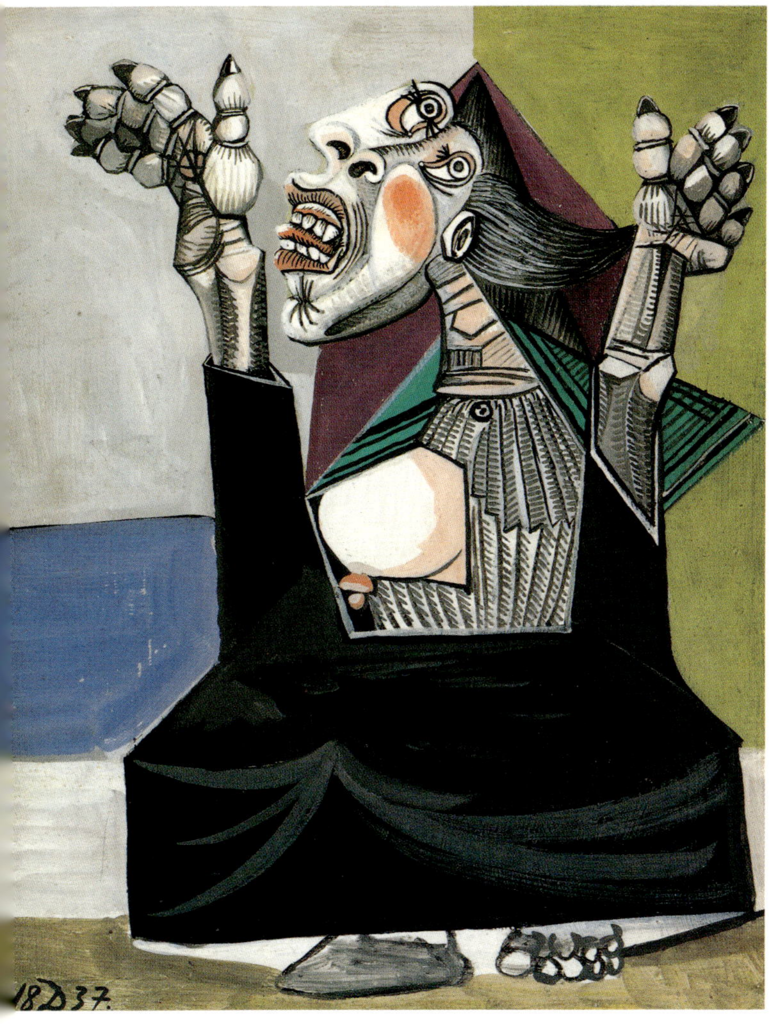

18.D.37.

Pablo Picasso
The Supplicant/Die Flehende, 1937
© Succession Picasso/VG Bild-Kunst, Bonn, 1993. Photo RMN, Paris

From the Prestel book/Aus dem Prestel-Buch:
Picasso-Museum Paris, The Masterpieces/Die Meisterwerke
(English and German editions) Prestel, Munich · New York

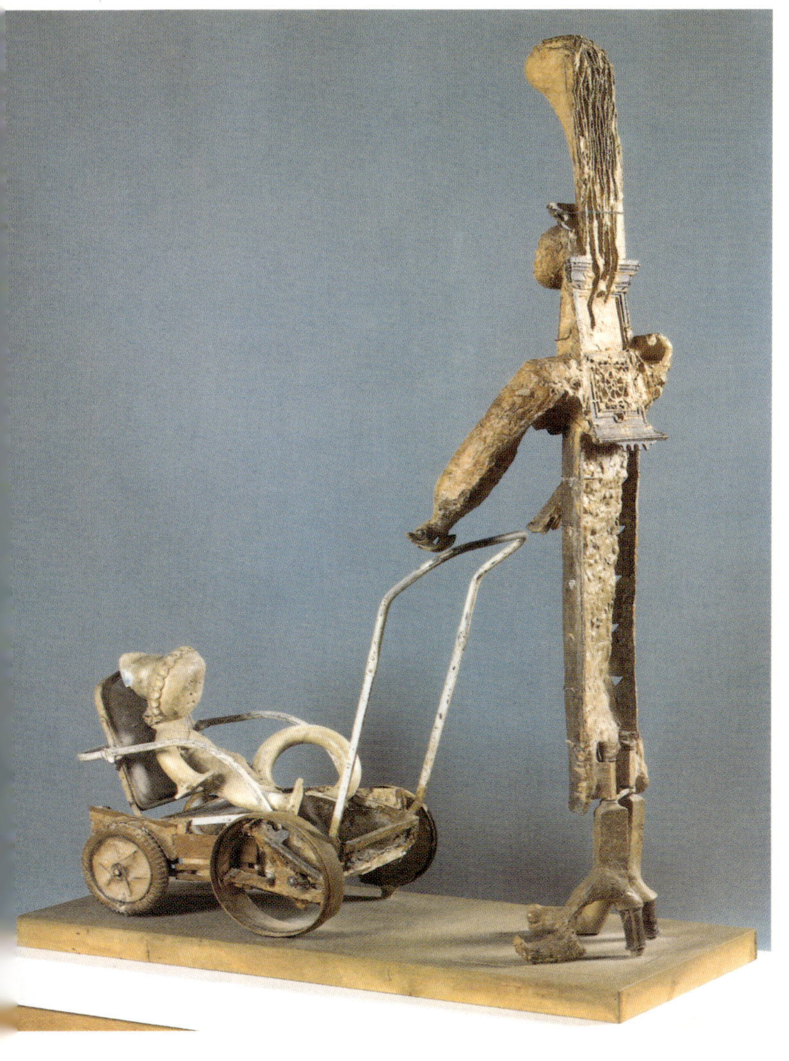

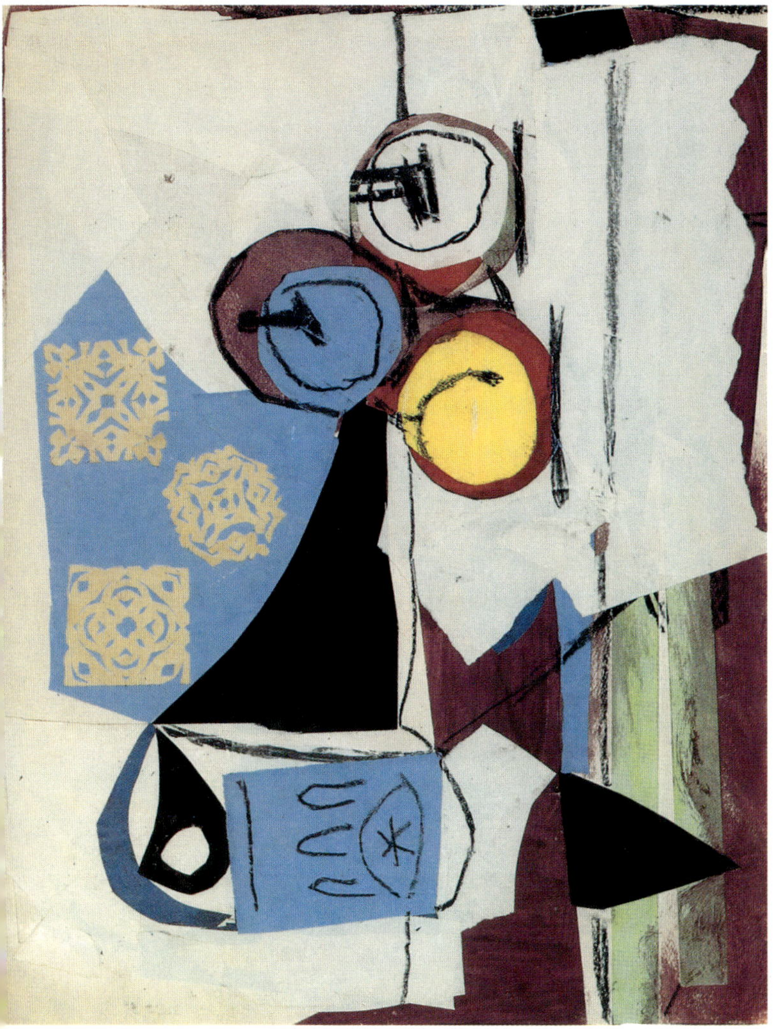

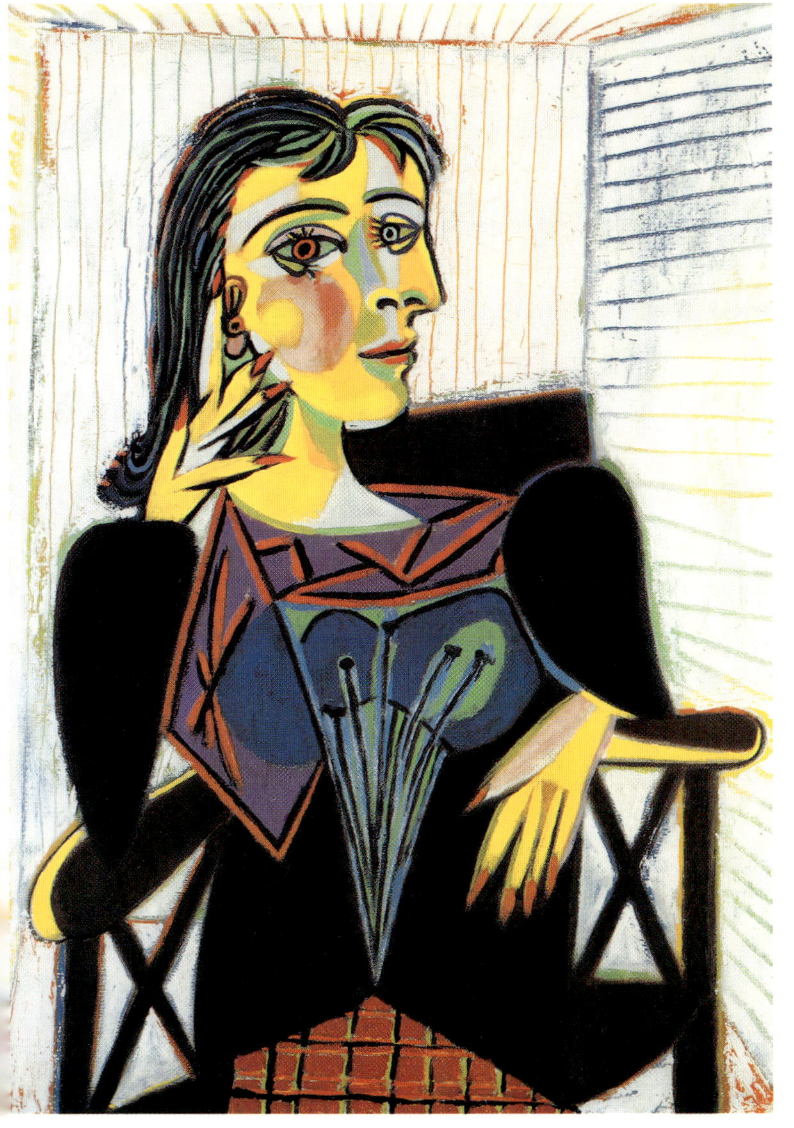

Pablo Picasso
Portrait of Dora Maar/Bildnis Dora Maar, 1937
© Succession Picasso/ VG Bild-Kunst. Bonn, 1993. Photo RMN. Paris

From the Prestel book /Aus dem Prestel-Buch:
Picasso-Museum Paris, The Masterpieces/Die Meisterwerke
(English and German editions) Prestel. Munich · New York

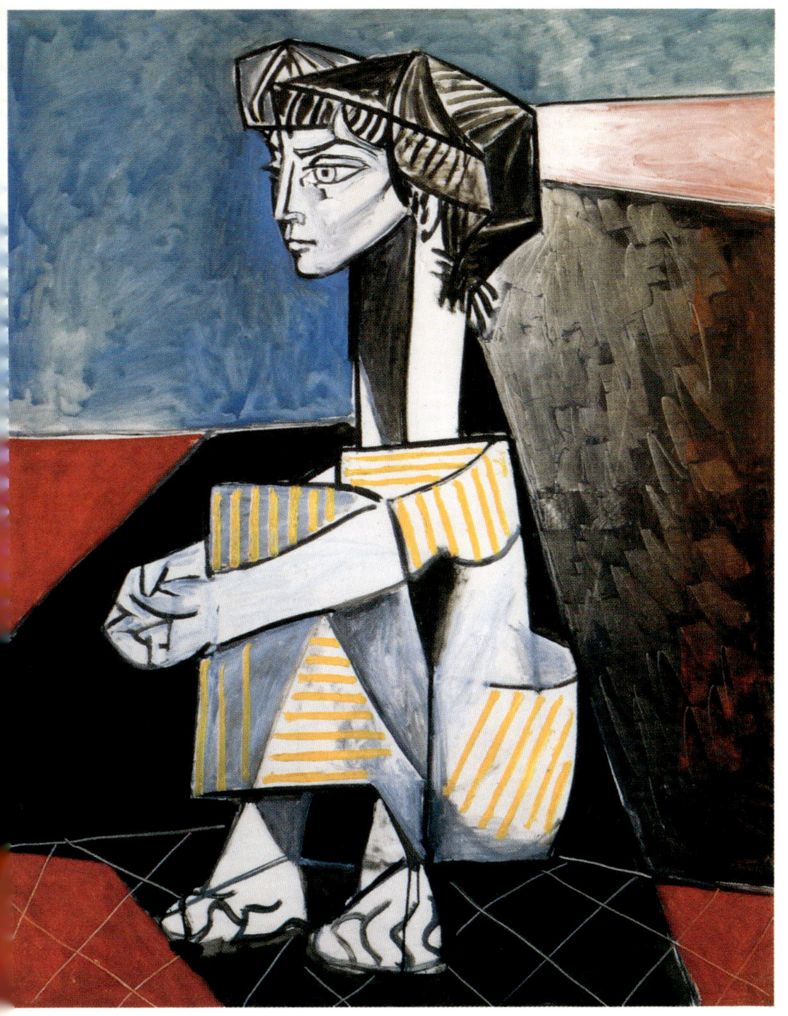

Pablo Picasso
Jacqueline with Crossed Hands/Jacqueline mit verschränkten Händen, 1954
© Succession Picasso/VG Bild-Kunst, Bonn, 1993, Photo RMN, Paris

From the Prestel book/Aus dem Prestel-Buch:
Picasso-Museum Paris, The Masterpieces/Die Meisterwerke
(English and German editions) Prestel, Munich · New York

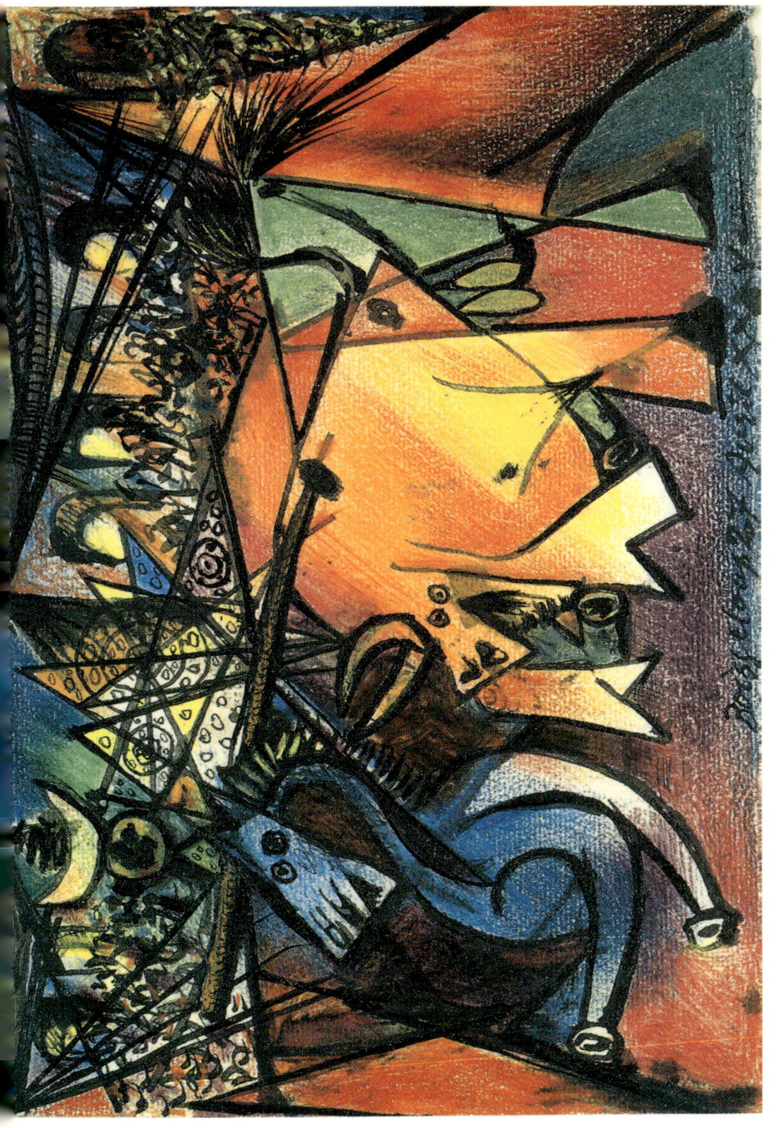

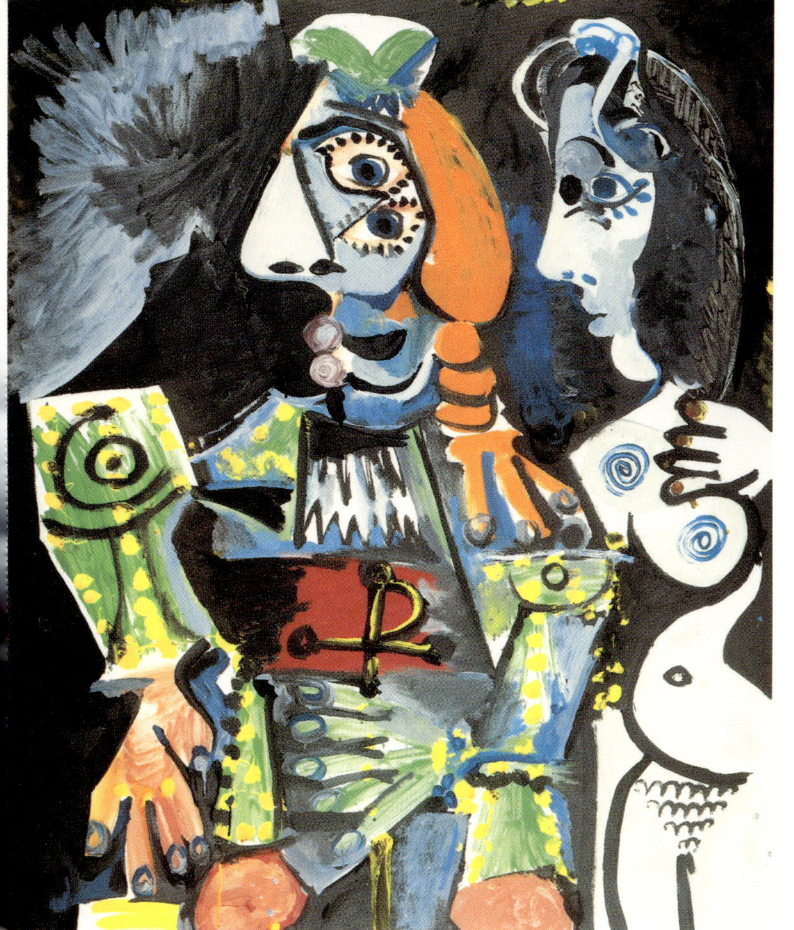

Pablo Picasso
Matador and Female Nude/Matador und weiblicher Akt, 1970
© Succession Picasso/VG Bild-Kunst, Bonn, 1993. Museum Ludwig, Cologne

From the Prestel book/Aus dem Prestel-Buch:
Picasso, The Ludwig Collection/Die Sammlung Ludwig
(English and German editions) Prestel, Munich · New York

Pablo Picasso
Susanna and the Two Old Men/Susanna und die beiden Alten, 1971
© Succession Picasso/VG Bild-Kunst, Bonn, 1993, Museum Ludwig, Cologne

From the Prestel book/Aus dem Prestel-Buch:
Picasso, The Ludwig Collection/Die Sammlung Ludwig
(English and German editions) Prestel, Munich · New York

Pablo Picasso

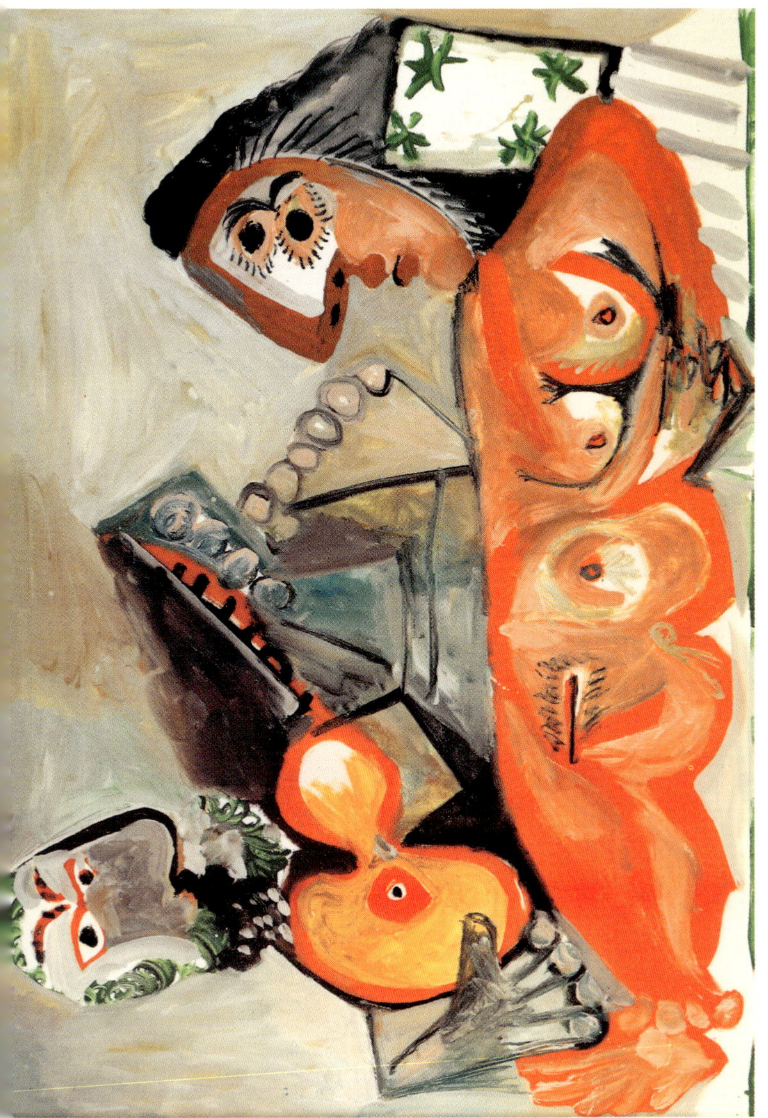

Reclining Nude and Man Playing the Guitar/Liegender Akt und Mann mit Gitarre, 1970
© Succession Picasso/VG Bild-Kunst, Bonn, 1993. Photo RMN, Paris

From the Prestel book/Aus dem Prestel-Buch:
Picasso-Museum Paris, The Masterpieces/Die Meisterwerke
(English and German editions) Prestel, Munich · New York